KINDNESS

Illustrations: Lindsey Sagar
Text: Eve Tombleson
Design: Rachel Baines

First American Edition 2023
Kane Miller, A Division of EDC Publishing

This book was conceived, created and produced by iSeek Ltd,
1A Stairbridge Court, Haywards Heath, West Sussex, RH17 5PA, UK
Copyright © iSeek Ltd 2022

All rights reserved, including the rights of reproduction
in whole or in part in any form.
For information contact:
Kane Miller, A Division of EDC Publishing
5402 S 122nd E Ave, Tulsa, OK 74146
www.kanemiller.com

Printed in China
1 2 3 4 5 6 7 8 9 10
ISBN: 978-1-68464-709-5

Let's get started

This book is about kindness. It is also about something called "mindfulness." Mindfulness is about paying attention to what you are doing and feeling. Being mindful to ourselves and others helps us to be kind.

The mindful activities in this book are designed to help you to feel good by making fun things for yourself and your friends and family.

How this book works

There are coloring, making, and writing activities in this book, as well as "doing" things, like a 30-day Kindness Challenge. You'll find paper templates to cut out on the pages just before or after the step-by-step instructions for each project. All the pages are perforated so you can tear them out to make filling them in and cutting out easier.

You may also need: pen, safety pin, glue, scissors, paintbrush, colored pencils, felt-tip pens, tape, colored thread, paint

Ask an adult to help with projects that use scissors.

Thinking about kindness

Have you ever thought about what kindness is?

Being kind isn't always about giving a gift or a treat. It can be as simple as noticing when a person needs a bit of help, perhaps holding open a door, or letting someone go ahead of you, or picking up something they have dropped. Even remembering to say "thank you" or giving a big smile can make others feel that they matter.

There are lots of ways to be kind. You can learn about them in this chapter.

Walk in someone's shoes

Have you heard this expression before? When something bad happens to someone, try to imagine how you would feel in a similar situation, as if you walked in their shoes. This is called "empathy."

Think about the last time you did something really kind for another person and how it made you feel good inside. Try to do that every day!

Kindness word search

You'll find 20 words for kindness in this word search. You can read across from left to right, or backward (from right to left), and either down (from top to bottom), or up (from bottom to top), so you need to look carefully.

You'll find that there are lots of words for kindness. They all mean something different. If you're not sure about a word, ask an adult to help explain it to you.

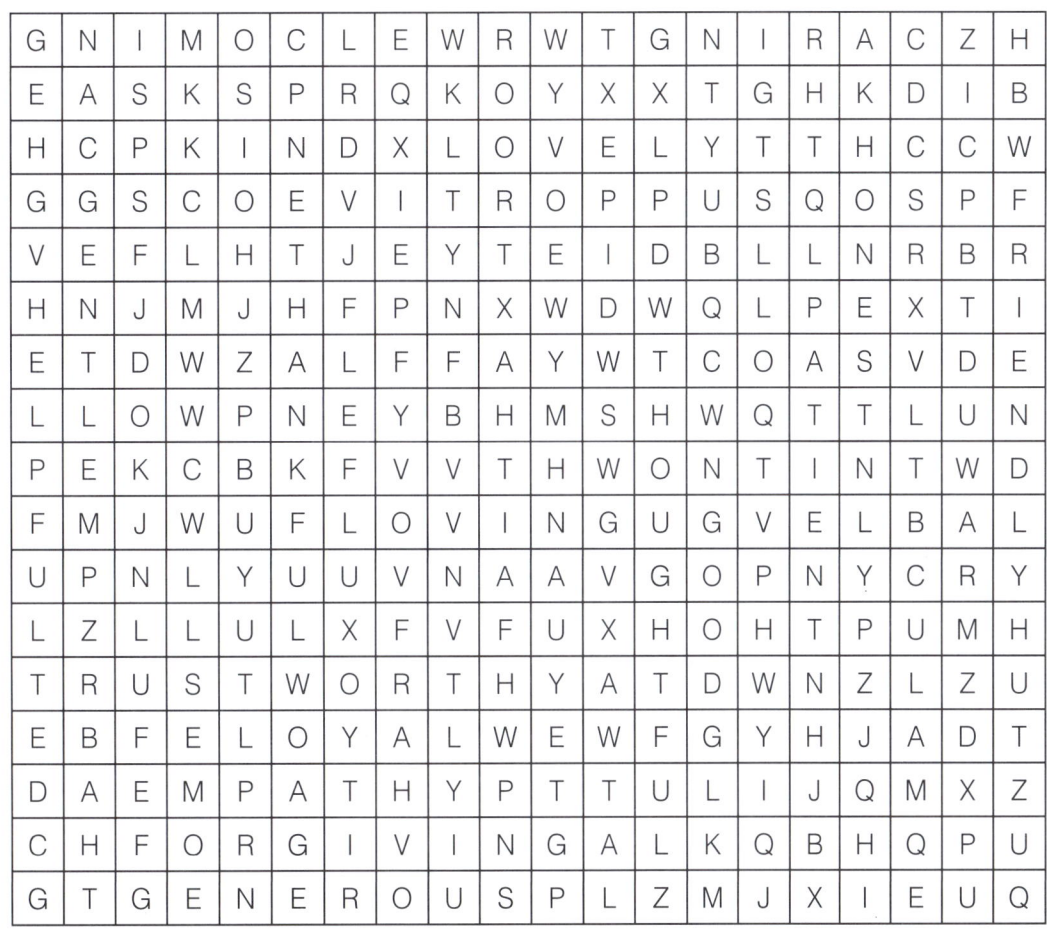

See if you can find all of these words.

Thankful, trustworthy, supportive, thoughtful, caring, loyal, loving, forgiving, friendly, lovely, kind, patient, welcoming, helpful, warm, good, honest, generous, empathy, gentle.

Word search answers

Here are the word search answers. Write in the boxes at the bottom of the page how you felt when someone was kind to you, and when someone was unkind to you.

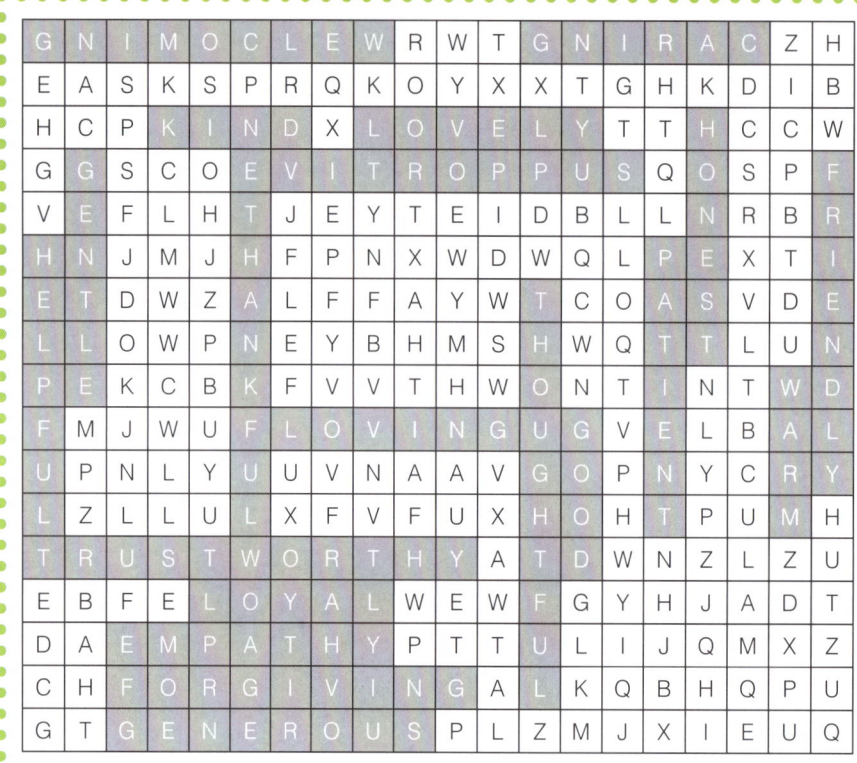

When someone was kind to me I felt:

....

....

....

When someone was unkind to me I felt:

....

....

....

What's up, tiger?

Cut out both sets of squares. Practice recognizing other people's feelings by matching the tiger's emotions to each situation.

Angry	Proud	Happy	Scared
Nervous	Sad	Excited	Jealous

1 They have a surprise waiting for them at home.
They are feeling..........

2 They received a gift.
They are feeling..........

3 Their best friend has moved away.
They are feeling..........

4 Their ice cream fell off the cone.
They are feeling..........

5 They are starting a new school.
They are feeling..........

6 They won the race.
They are feeling..........

7 They don't like the dark.
They are feeling..........

8 Their friend has a new puppy.
They are feeling..........

What's up, tiger?

Cut out the squares. Write an example of when you felt each emotion on the top squares. Then write how you could help a friend who is feeling the emotions on the bottom squares.

I felt angry when...	I felt proud when...	I felt happy when...	I felt scared when...
I felt nervous when...	I felt sad when...	I felt excited when...	I felt jealous when...
I can help a nervous friend by...	I can help a scared friend by...	I can help a sad friend by...	I can help an angry friend by...
I can help a happy friend by...	I can help a jealous friend by...	I can help an excited friend by...	I can help a proud friend by...

Empathy

Empathy is important because it helps you to see things from another person's point of view, and this means that you can really understand how that person is feeling.

Color in this heart.

Test your manners

When you practice good manners, you are showing people that you care about their feelings. How good are your manners? Take the quiz!

You need:
- Scissors
- Colored pencils
- Pen

①

Color in the animals. Cut along the dotted lines.

② Complete the sentences using one of the phrases.

- Sorry
- Sharing
- Please
- Are you OK?
- Help
- Thank you

Why do you think it is important to have good manners?

....
....
....
....

When you ask for something you say...

When you receive something you say...

If you make someone sad or upset you say...

If someone is scared you offer them...

If someone is having a bad day you ask...

Letting someone use something of yours is...

Pick a number

Inspire random acts of kindness with this fun fortune-telling game.

You need:
- Scissors
- Colored pencils
- Pen

❷

Write one kind act in each of the triangles and color it. You could copy the ones in the picture or make up your own.

❶

Cut out the square on the next page.

❸

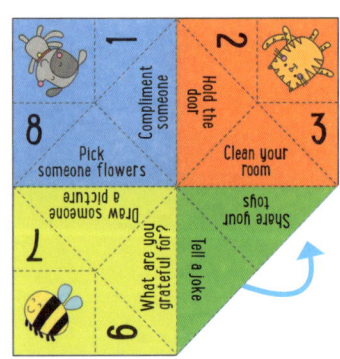

Fold each of the four corners into the center.

❹

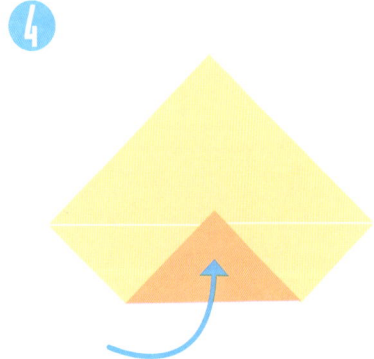

Turn over and fold the corners into the center again.

❺

Turn over again, pop it up, and then it's time to play.

How to play

Put one finger into each pocket and ask a friend for a number. Open and close the fortune-teller that many times.

What's the act of kindness for today?

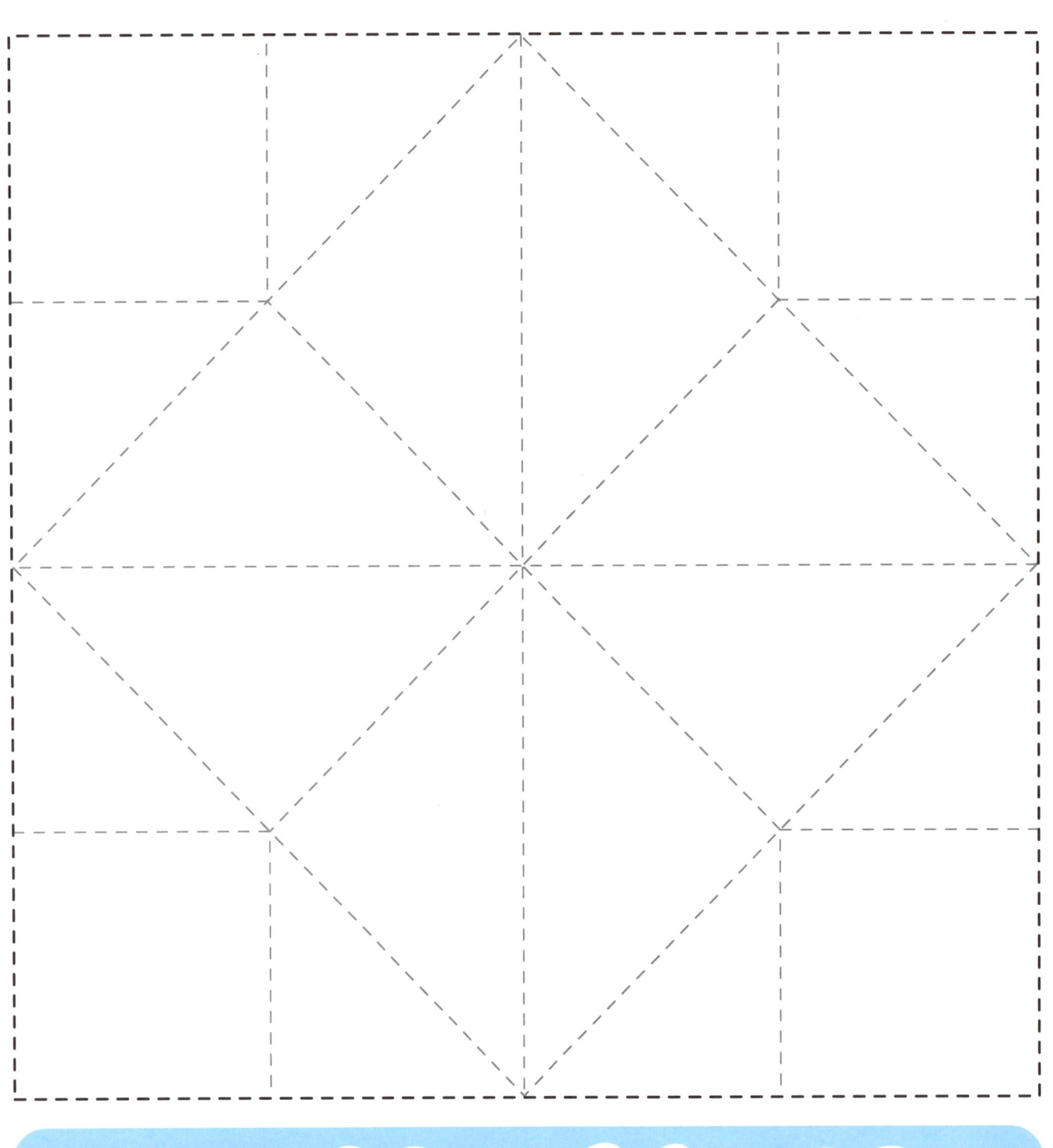

Kind thought of the day

One kind word can change someone's day.
What's your kind word for today?

....

Look after yourself

Kindness is not just thinking about others, it is also about YOU caring for YOU and looking after yourself. This can be as simple as remembering to brush your teeth twice a day and eating healthy food.

It can also be about looking after your own feelings and understanding what makes you feel good and what doesn't.

Below are examples of things you may enjoy that make you feel good. There may be many more that you can think of.

A simple way to feel better if you're feeling worried or scared is to "square" breathe. Breathe in for 4 seconds, hold for 4 seconds, breathe out for 4 seconds, and hold for 4 seconds. Do this two times. How do you feel now?

Here are some other ideas.

Today I will...

Mind
be creative
read my book
learn something new

Body
eat healthily
exercise
relax

Spirit
sing a happy song
help others
dance

Heart
laugh
have fun
play with my friends

Self-care is in the air

Self-care is about being kind to ourselves. When we are kind to ourselves it is easier to be kind to others.

You need:
- Scissors
- Pen
- Tape
- Colored pencils
- String

1

Color in the hot-air balloons and cut them out.

2

Write on each balloon something kind you can do for yourself.

3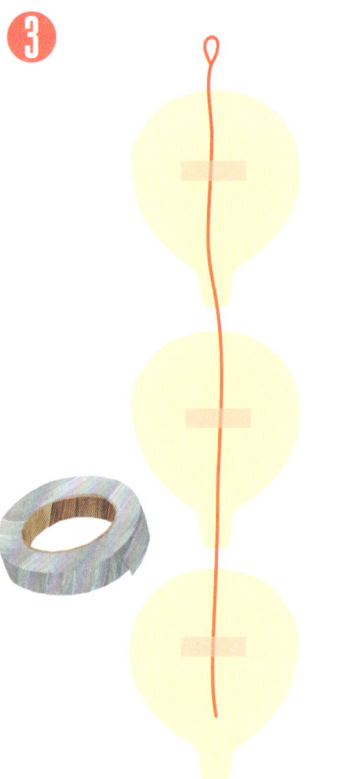

Tape a piece of string to the back of the balloons to join them together.

4

Hang up in your bedroom.

Self-care ideas
- Listen to happy music
- Do something fun
- Be creative
- Read a favorite book
- Spend time outside
- Clean your room
- Wear a favorite color

Positivity bracelets

Make yourself a bracelet with a positive message to yourself on one side. For example, you could write: "I am brave," or "I am responsible," or "I am trying my best."

GLUE	I am
GLUE	I am
GLUE	I am
GLUE	I am
GLUE	I am
GLUE	I am
GLUE	I am

Positivity bracelets

On the other side, write a secret message just for you, such as: "I am the only me in the whole world. Yippee!"

GLUE	Secret message
GLUE	Secret message
GLUE	Secret message
GLUE	Secret message
GLUE	Secret message
GLUE	Secret message
GLUE	Secret message

I am thankful for...

Feeling grateful can help us to become more positive.

Draw a person you are thankful for.

What was the best part of your week?

Who made you happy today, and why?

What are you going to enjoy doing today?

Give yourself a bear hug

Are you a hugger? Do you like receiving bear hugs? Most of us do. Enjoy big hugs with Bernie the Bear.

You need:
- Scissors
- Pen
- Glue

1
Cut out the bear, arms, and tummy pocket.

2
Glue the tummy pocket onto the bear. Leave the top open.

3
Glue the end of each arm onto the body.

4
Cut out the hearts.

5

On each heart write something kind about yourself.

6
Put all of your hearts in the bear's pocket and give yourself a big bear hug.

Kind thoughts lead to kind actions

Color in the picture on the next page.

Color in this page.

Peacock of gratitude

Thinking about things you are grateful for can help you to feel good!

You need:
- Scissors
- Pen
- Glue
- Colored pencils

1. Color in the peacock.

2. Cut out the peacock and its tail feathers.

3. On each tail feather write something you are grateful for.

(sunny days, pets, clean water, family)

4. Glue the feathers around the peacock.

Offer to make a gratitude peacock for a friend, and find out what makes them happy!

Be kind to yourself and think happy thoughts.

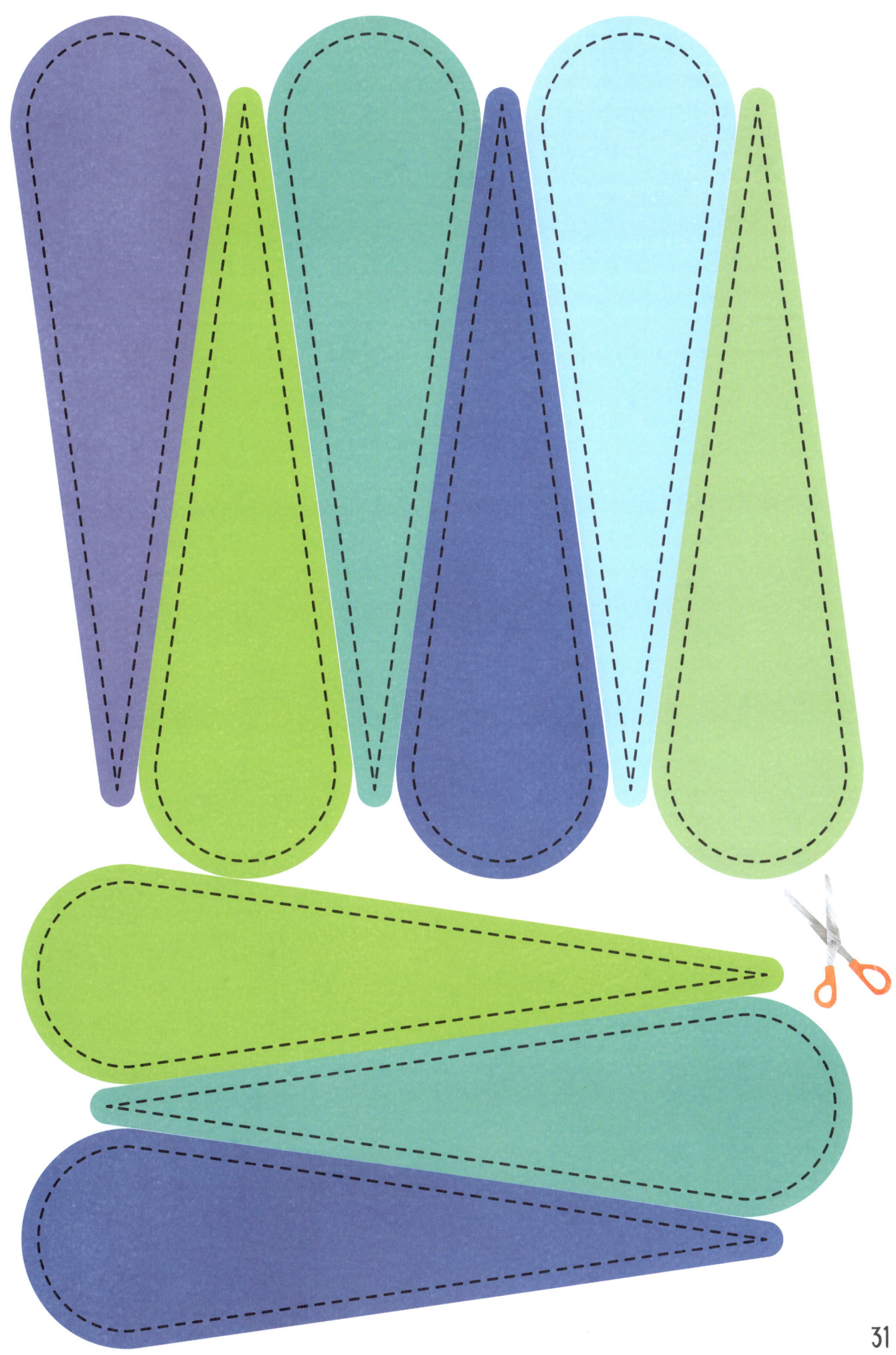

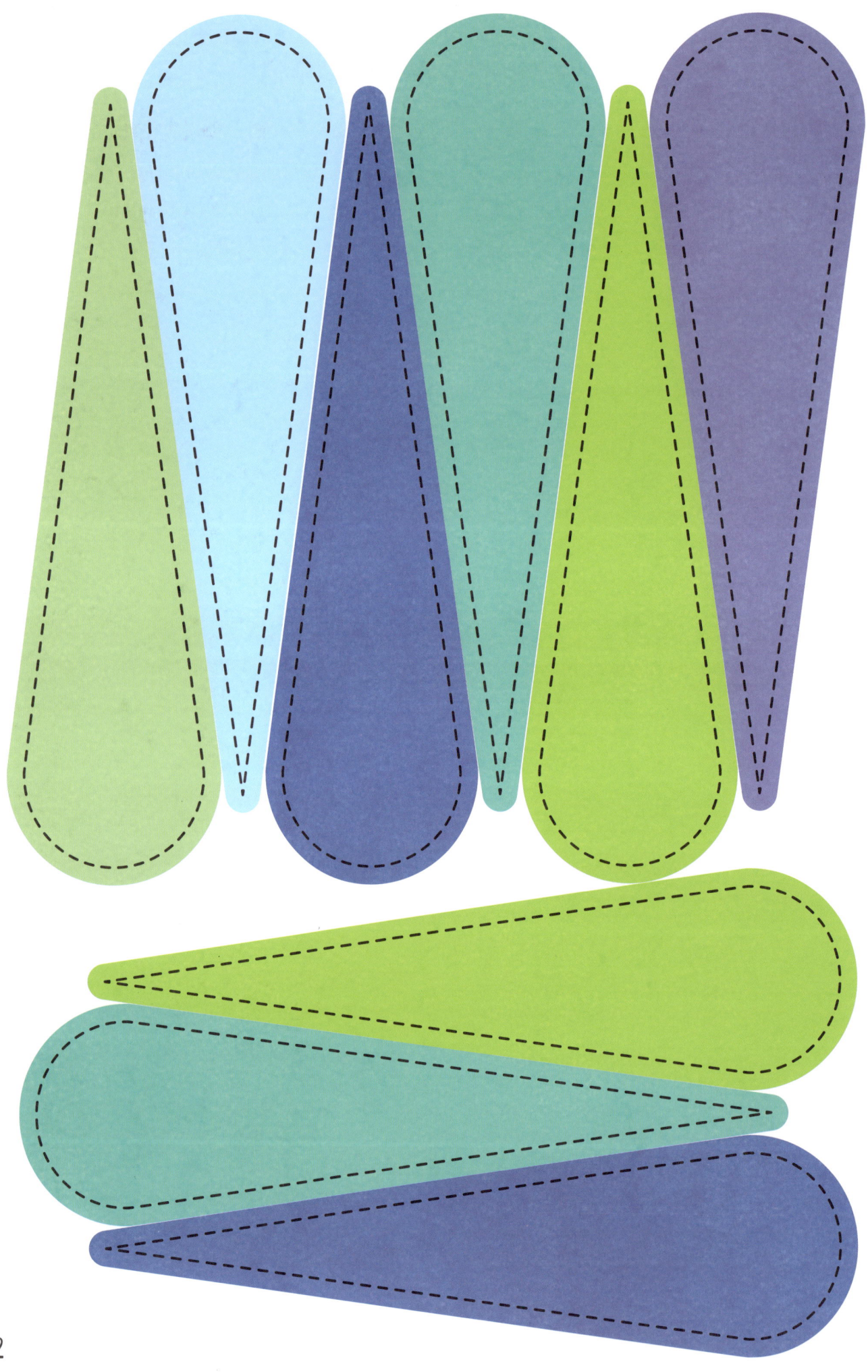

Box of happiness

Make this colorful box and fill it with happy and positive notes to yourself.

You need:
- Scissors
- Pen
- Glue
- Colored pencils or felt-tip pens

❶

Cut out the box, the flower head, and the rectangles.

❷

Color in the box template and flower. Felt-tip pens or colored pencils work best.

You can make a bigger box and fill it with things that make you feel good, such as your favorite photos.

❸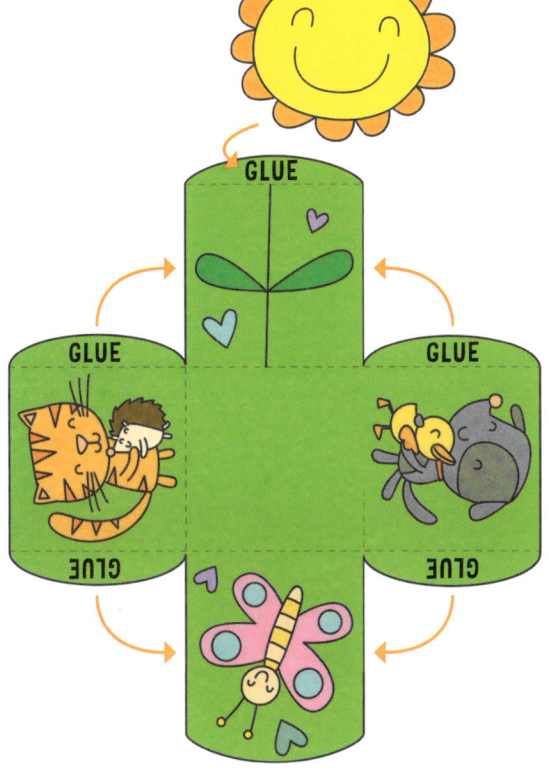

Fold in the sides and glue the tabs. Glue the flower head to the box.

33

4 On each of the rectangles write down something that makes you feel good.

I like....	I am proud of myself for...	I did a good job when...

5

Now put all the happy notes into the box.

You could also make a box for a friend and fill it with happy memories of the times you've spent together.

Kindness to others

Being a kind person means that you care about other people's feelings. Without kindness, people can be hurtful. Bullying someone is an example of hurtful behavior.

You can often tell how a person is feeling by the look on their face.

In this chapter we show you lots of different ways to be kind to others, from making a friendship bracelet as a gift, to helping a parent make dinner.

Do you remember our tiger?
Can you write the correct emotion beneath each face?

....

Let's take turns!

Drops of kindness

A drop of kindness goes a long way and helps your friendships to grow.

You need:
- Scissors
- Pen
- Glue
- Colored pencils or felt-tip pens

1

Cut out the watering can pieces and the raindrops.

2

Glue the sides together, but leave the top open to form a pocket.

3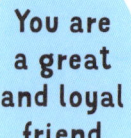

- You are very funny and kind
- You are creative and make cool art
- You are a great and loyal friend
- You give the best hugs
- You are a great listener
- You always share

On each raindrop, write a kind and positive message.

4

Put the raindrops in the pocket. When you spot someone who is sad, water them with a kindness raindrop.

You can decorate your watering can using felt-tip pens or colored pencils. You could try stars, stripes, or spots.

Kind thought of the day

I say my words in a kind way.

Kind thought of the day

I am happy when I am kind.

small steps to kindness

Think about the times you have been mean to someone. You can turn it around!

You need:
- Scissors
- Pen

①

Cut out the cloud and sun shapes.

②

I shouted when I lost the game.

On each cloud, write examples of when you have been unkind.

③

I can help my friend if she falls over.

On each sun, write how you could be kinder in the future.

43

small steps to kindness

You can use the backs of the suns and clouds, too.

If you are being unkind, ask yourself, why? Are you tired or hungry? Did you find something difficult or feel it was unfair?

Write why in the space below.

I am being unkind because....................

....

....

....

Kindness award

This is the template for the kindness award.

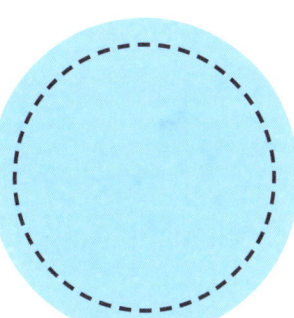
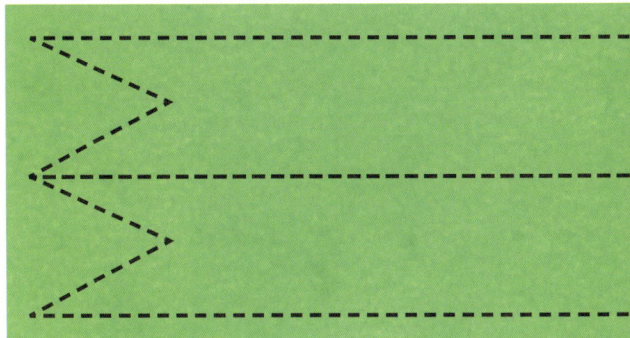

Kindness award

This is the template for the kindness award.

Kindness award

This is the template for a second kindness award.

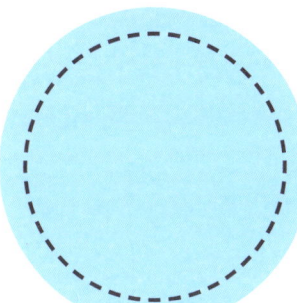
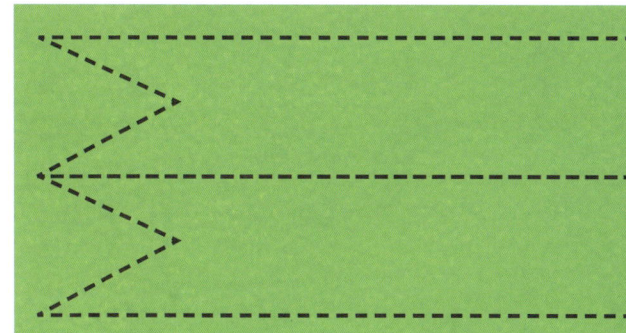

Kindness award

This is the template for a second kindness award.

You need:
- Scissors
- Glue
- Tape
- Safety pin

1
Cut out the rectangles.

2
Concertina fold each rectangle.

3
Fold each concertina in half, and glue together the middle to form a semicircle.

4
Then, glue both pieces together to make a circle.

5
Turn over and glue the small blue circle onto the back.

6
Open the safety pin. Glue the ribbons onto the blue circle, securing the safety pin in place.

7
Turn over and glue the big blue circle onto the front.

Kitchen kindness

Keep a record of your helpfulness on a chart.
You can use this one or make your own.

Responsibility	Sun	Mon	Tues	Wed	Thurs	Fri	Sat
I helped with the food shopping.							
I helped put the food away.							
I set the table.							
I got the drinks.							
I helped rinse the plates.							
I helped to clear the table.							

Remember that being responsible is good for you, and also for the people around you.

Kitchen Kindness

Color in and cut out an ice cream scoop every time you help in the kitchen. Then glue it to the cone on the chart.

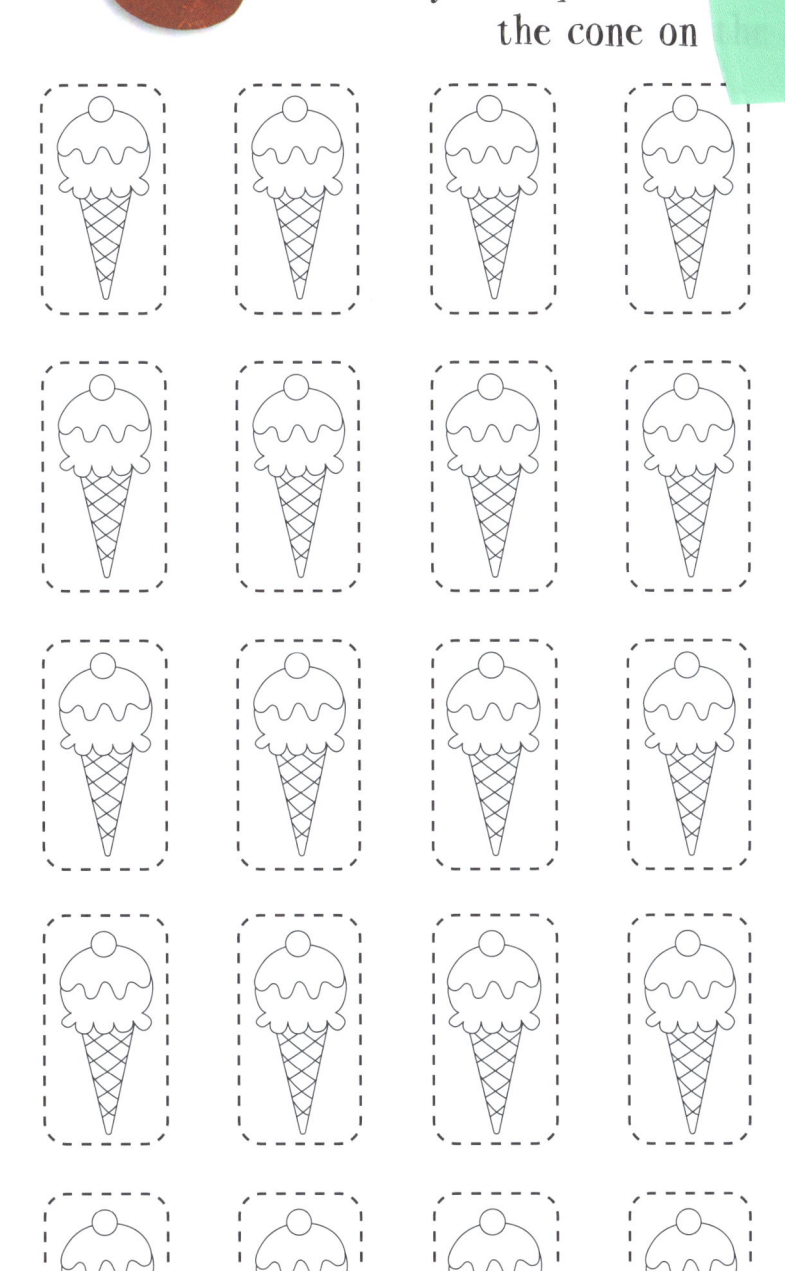

Kitchen kindness

Glue your ice cream cone onto the chart on the previous page.

Remembering game

Cut out these characters. Look at the pictures and read the names. Try to remember both.

Alex

George

Robin

Amelia

Harry

Emma

Mia

Oliver

Noah

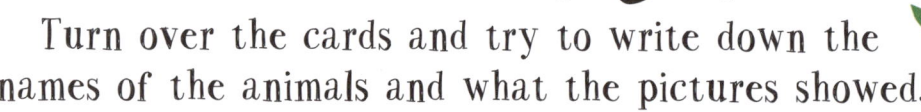

Remembering game

Turn over the cards and try to write down the names of the animals and what the pictures showed.

| Whose ice cream melted? | Who brought a present for you? | Who sent a kind letter? |

| Who fell over and hurt their leg? | Who wore new red boots in the rain? | Who made an origami bird in after-school club? |

| Who loves dancing? | Who had a new toy to share? | Who loves painting and drawing? |

Friendship bracelet

Make someone's day extra special by making them a friendship bracelet!

- A good friend is someone you enjoy being with.
- A good friend can help when you are feeling upset.
- A good friend is someone you share secrets with.

You need:

- Scissors
- Colored thread x3. Each color must be at least 12 ft. long.

1 Cut around the circle on the next page. Glue it to a piece of thin card stock, then cut it out neatly.

2  Cut eight .4 in. slits equally around the circle. Ask an adult to poke a hole through the middle.

3  Cut each color thread into four 3 ft. lengths.

4 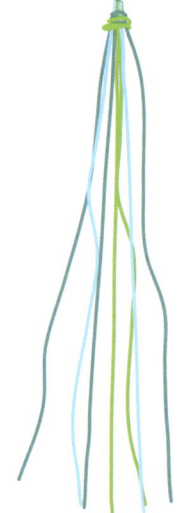 Gather together seven of the lengths and tie a double knot at the end.

5  Push the knot through the middle and slot one thread length into each slit.

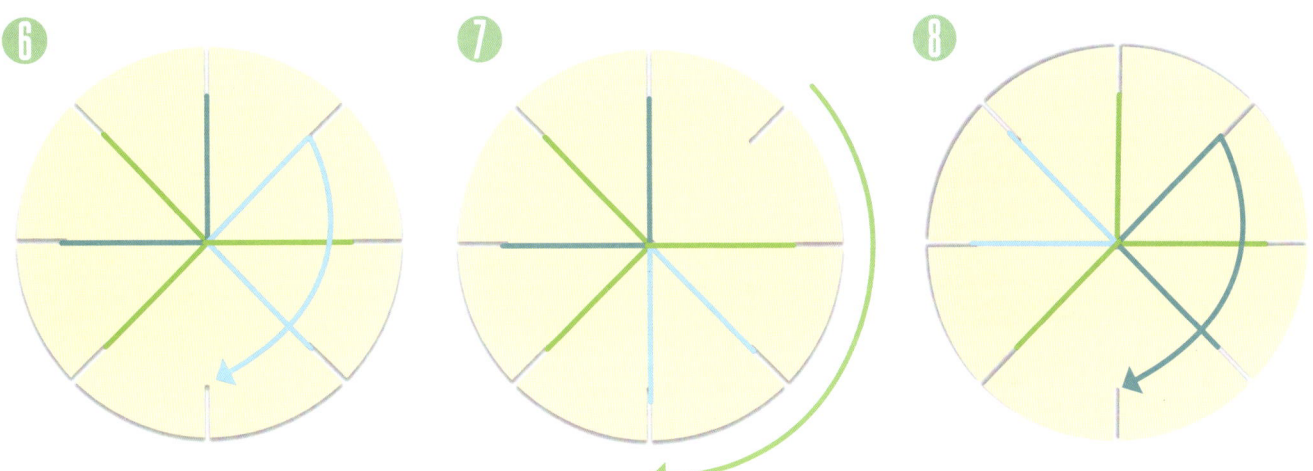

6 Hold the circle with one hand and take the third thread and slot it into the bottom slit.

7 It should look like this. Turn the wheel around so the empty slit is at the bottom again.

8 Now keep repeating steps 5 to 7 until a bracelet starts to form. Gently pull through the woven bracelet as it emerges.

Tip: Make sure you untangle the thread on the other side as you go so it doesn't get knotted.

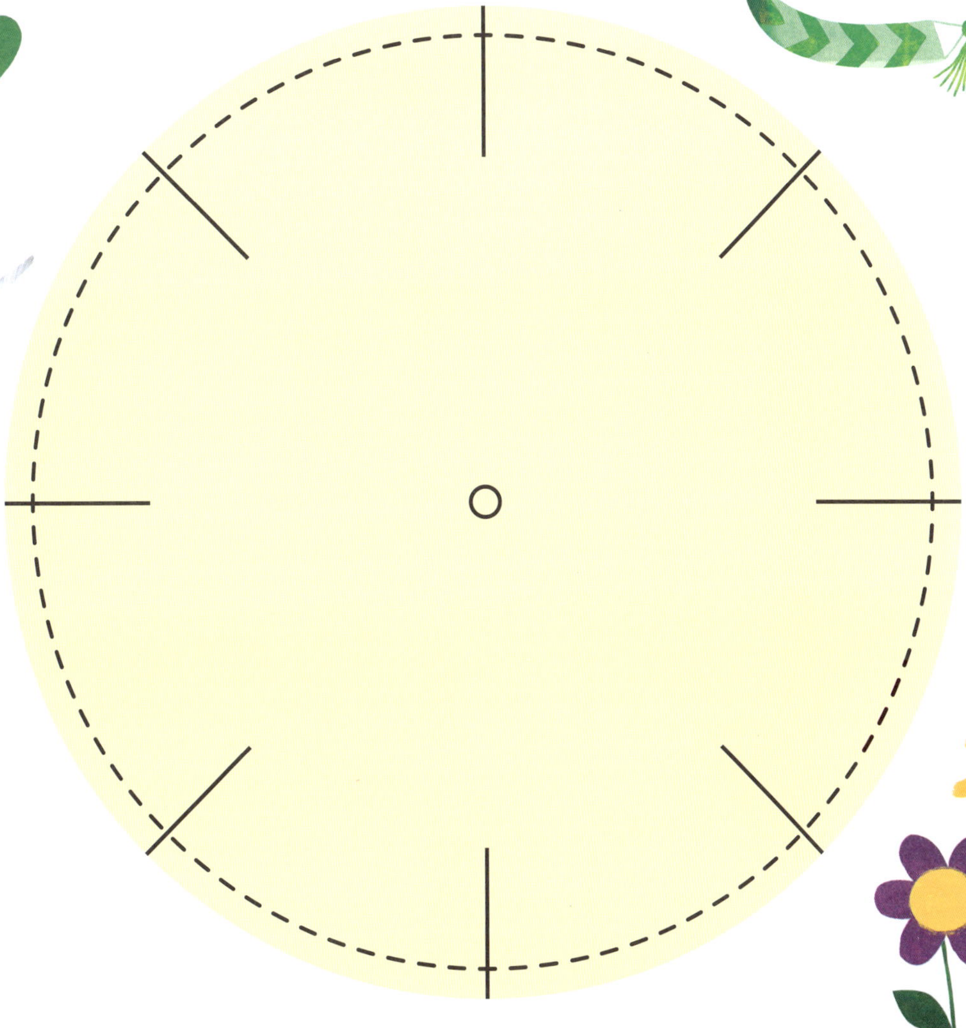

57

Kindness to animals

We should not only show kindness to people, but also to animals. We know our pets need us to care for them, but wild animals also need our help. They need protecting from hunters and from people who destroy the habitats in which they live.

Animals feel pain just like people, so be gentle when you pet them – and never tease them.

This chapter has lots of activities to show how much you care about nature.

Show kindness to our planet

We need to do more to save our planet.

We must preserve the rain forests and oceans, and stop polluting the Earth and making it hotter. Caring more for our planet not only helps animals to survive, it helps us too. Plants such as trees and kelp (seaweed) produce oxygen that we all need to breathe.

What could you do to help the planet?

1. Stop using plastic
2. Recycle old clothes and toys
3. Volunteer to pick up litter in your neighborhood
4. Fundraise for a wildlife charity
5. Make a wildlife garden
6. Plant a tree

Color in this page.
I am kind

to our planet and its animals

Tree of kindness

Make this tree of kindness to remind you to be kind to nature.

You need:
- Scissors
- Pen
- Glue

1

Cut out the treetop and trunk.

2

Glue the tree trunk to the leaves.

3

Cut out the acorn shapes and write down an act of kindness on each one.

4

Glue the acorns to the tree.

Share your tree of kindness with friends. It may inspire them!

Sometimes we get things wrong and we are unkind. There's no need to worry. Apologize to the person you were unkind to, and then think about how you can behave better in the future.

If you sometimes wake up feeling grumpy, forgive yourself and leap into a kinder future.

Leap of kindness

Jump into kindness with these origami frogs.

1. Cut out the rectangles to make two frogs.

2. Fold as shown. Push in the sides. The top will pull down as you do this.

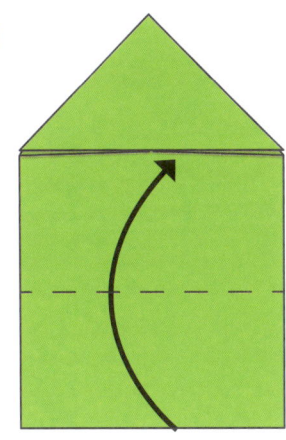

3. Turn over, then fold up the bottom edge.

4. Fold up two little triangles at the top as shown here.

5. Fold over the two sides to meet in the center by tucking them under the little triangles.

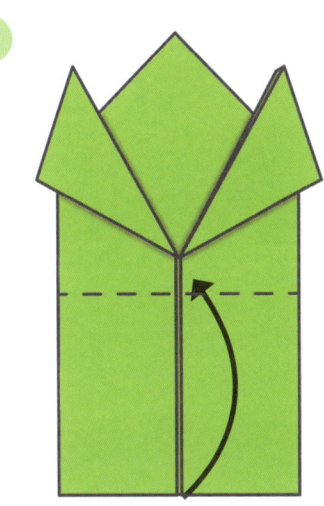

6. Fold up the bottom edge.

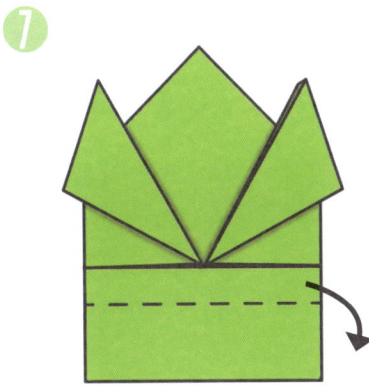

7. Fold the top edge back.

8. Draw a happy face on your frog.

Press down on the back of the head to make the frog leap.

Help the Earth

Make this 3D model to hang up in your bedroom.

You need:
- Scissors
- Colored pencils
- Pen
- Glue

①

Cut out the globe template.

②

Color in the sea and land using green and blue colored pencils.

③

Cut out one of the green strips and glue it onto tab 11.

④

Fold the tabs down along the dotted lines and glue in order, starting at 1.

⑤

Cut out the heart shapes.

⑥

On each heart, write something you can do to help the planet.

⑦

Glue each heart onto the strip.

⑧

Cut out another strip of paper and make a loop. Stick it to the top of the model.

Plant diary

Caring for living things, like plants, is a way of being kind and mindful toward the Earth. Next time you grow something, fill in this sheet.

My plant looks like

My plant is called a

Facts about my plant

My plant needs

Other information

Bee-kind finger puppets

Make a pair of finger puppets - one for you and one for a friend. Have fun playing together.

You need:
- Scissors
- Glue

1.
Cut out the two yellow circles. Ask an adult to cut the two finger holes in the bigger circle.

2.
Cut out the two blue circles for the wings.

3.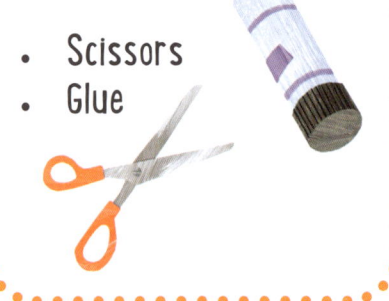
Glue the wings to the big circle to make the bee's body. Glue the head so that it overlaps the body.

Bees are very important to the health of planet Earth. They pollinate plants, many of which we grow for food. One way you can help bees is to fundraise for an environmental charity.

4.
Cut out the two small black strips for the antennae and glue onto the head.

Repeat the steps to make one for your friend!

74

Animal research

Paying attention to animals is a way of being kind toward the Earth. Find out some facts about your favorite animal and write them here.

My animal looks like

My animal is called

Facts about my animal

My animal's habitat

Other information

Butterfly gliders

Butterflies are beautiful! Make these paper ones to show your appreciation.

You need:
- Scissors
- Colored pencils
- Glue
- Tape

1

Cut out the butterfly pieces.

2

Color in each of the pieces.

3

Cut down the center dotted line.

4

Slot the body and wings together. Add tape to secure if you need to.

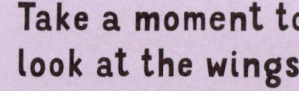

Take a moment to look at the wings.

Have you ever looked at a real butterfly's wings? They are delicate, with beautiful patterns.

5

Glue an antenna onto each side of the head and fold out.

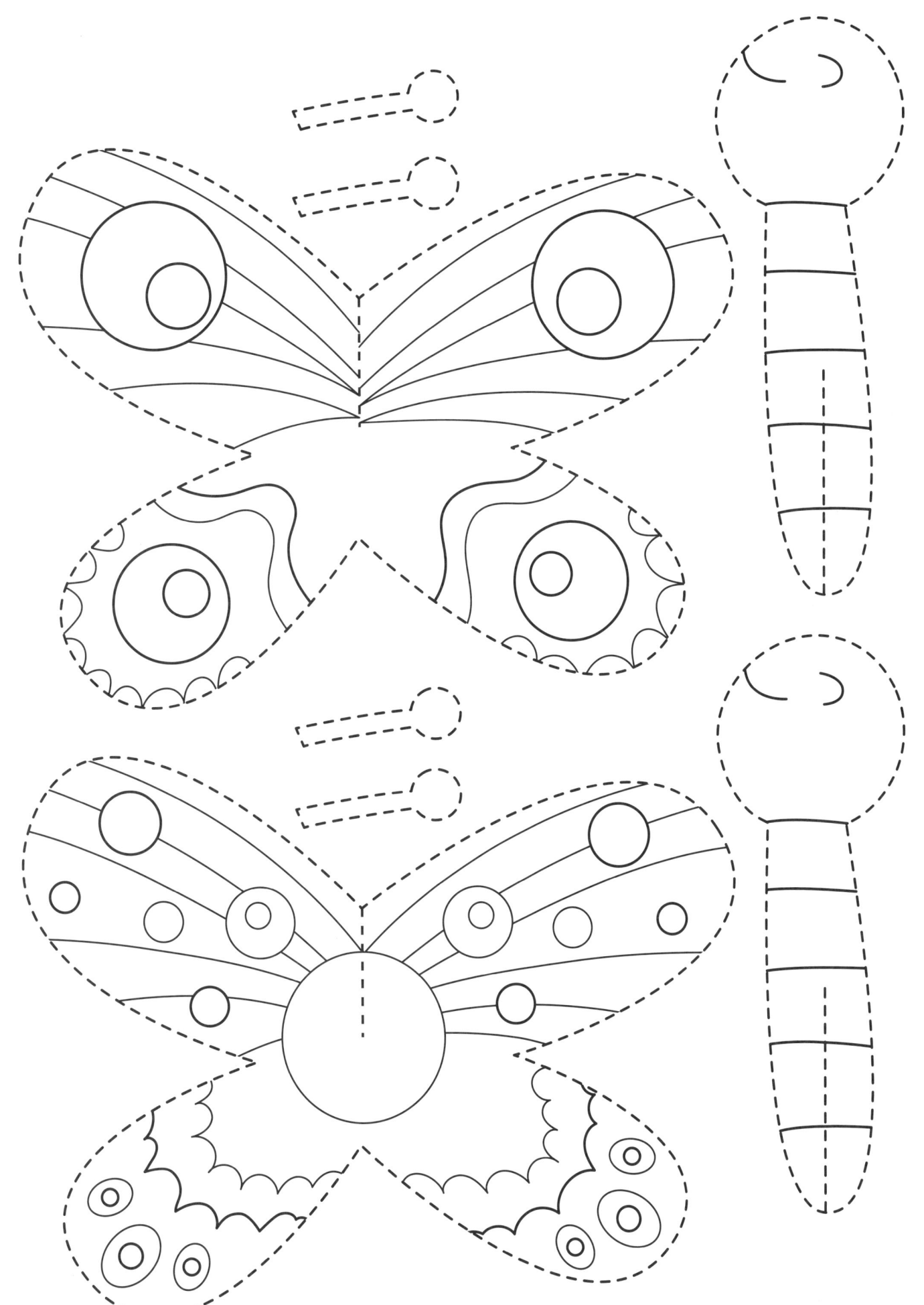

Nature notes

Make this koala box and fill it with notes that show how you value nature and the animals and plants around you.

You need:
- Scissors
- Pen
- Glue
- Colored pencils or felt-tip pens

1

Cut out the box, the koala's head, and the rectangles.

2

Color in the box and head. Felt-tip pens or colored pencils work best.

3

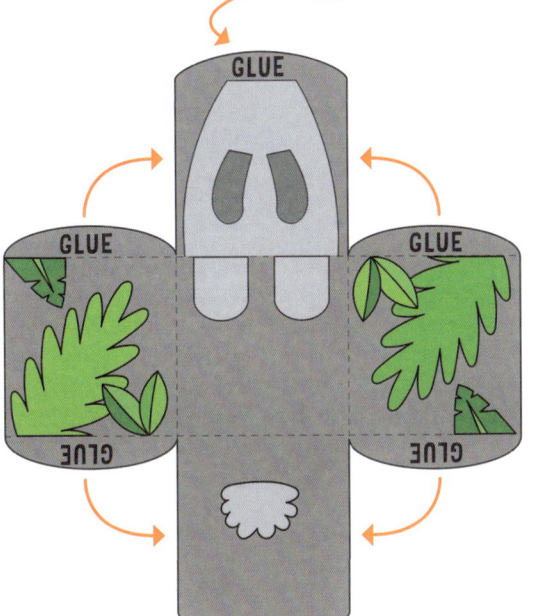

Tip:
Don't forget to cut around the koala's feet and fold them out! You may need adult help.

Fold along the dotted lines and glue the tabs and koala's head to the box.

4 On each rectangle write down something about your love of nature.

| My favorite bug is.... | I look after nature by... | I respect all animals, even scary ones like... |

| I help look after my pet by... | | |

5

Put all the kindness messages in the box.

How can you be kinder to animals?

We share the Earth, so we must learn to look after its animals.

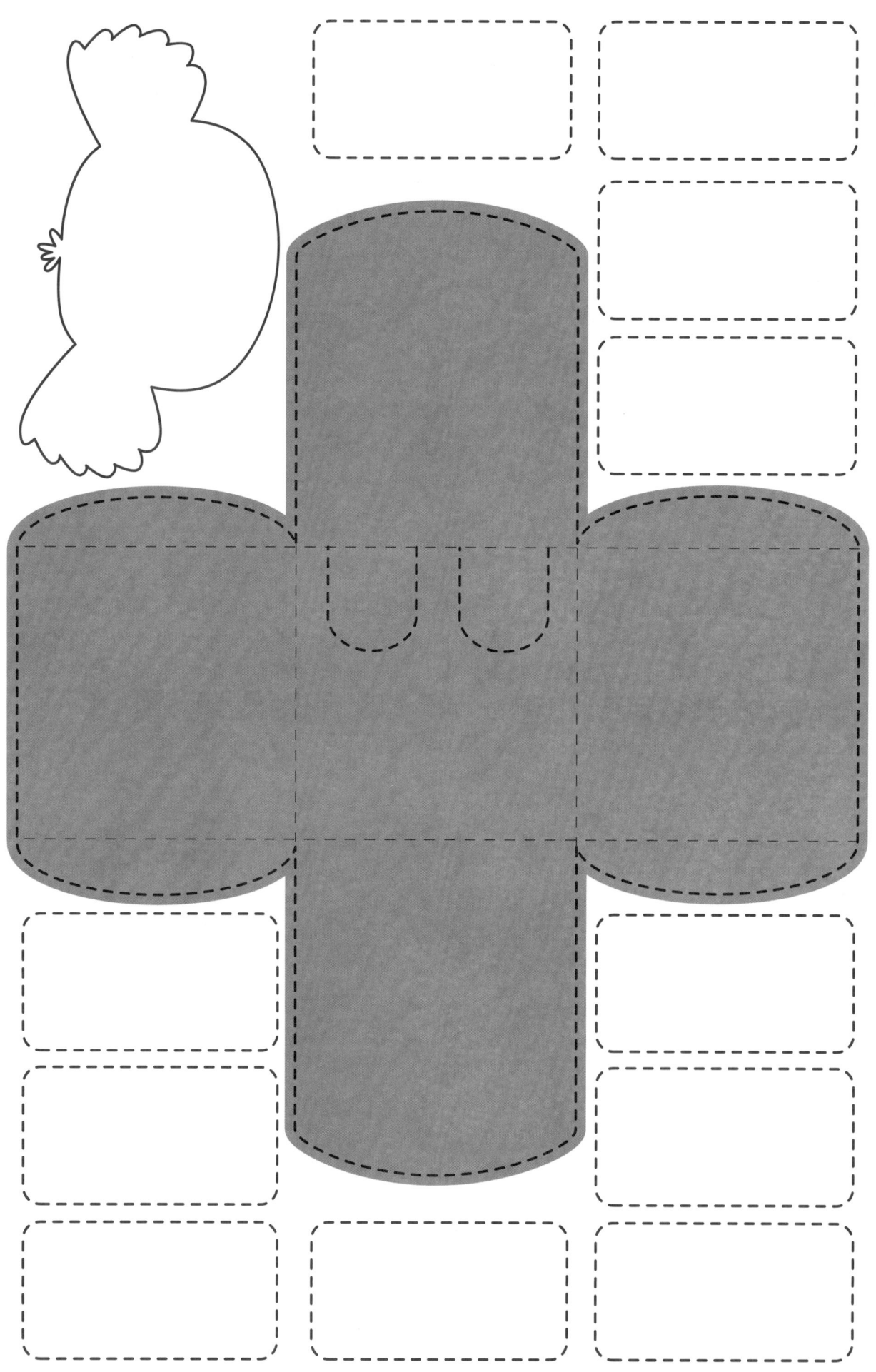

84

Bringing it all together

You've learned a lot about kindness, and hopefully had fun doing the activities in this book. Use this space to write down some of the things you've discovered.

Which activities were the most fun?

....

Which activities made you think about how kind you are?

....

Have you tried to be kinder?

....

Have you noticed a difference in how people behave toward you?

....

Can you make a list of all the kinds things you've been inspired to do?

....

....

....

....

Kind thought of the day
I choose to be kind.

30 days of kindness

Look at the activities and do one a day for 30 days. Have fun!

Do the activity and then cut out the matching picture.

The pictures are numbered 1–30.

Underneath each one, write how you feel after completing the activity.

Say thank you

I feel.................
....

Compliment someone

I feel.................
....

Hug someone

I feel.................
....

Help clean up at home or school

I feel.................
....

Listen

I feel.................
....

Share your toys

I feel.................
....

Make a gift

I feel.................
....

Read to someone

I feel.................
....

Write a kind note

I feel.................
....

Offer to help

I feel.................
....

**After the first 10 days give yourself a treat!
What did you give yourself?**

....

Cheer up someone	**Plant a flower**	**Eat healthily**	**Let someone go first**
I feel...............	I feel...............	I feel...............	I feel...............

High-five someone	**Water the plants**	**Take turns**	**Do a chore**
I feel...............	I feel...............	I feel...............	I feel...............

Say "good morning"	**Ask "how are you?"**	**Be creative**	**Help someone**
I feel...............	I feel...............	I feel...............	I feel...............

Make someone smile	Recycle	Make a new friend	Tell a joke
I feel....................	I feel....................	I feel....................	I feel....................

Be nice to bugs	Paint with a friend	Make a card	Celebrate kindness
I feel....................	I feel....................	I feel....................	I feel....................

What other activities can you think of? Write them down here.

Color in this page.

Kindness koala

You've learned so much about how to promote kindness in yourself and others. Let's finish with a mindful activity.

1
Cut out the gray square opposite.

2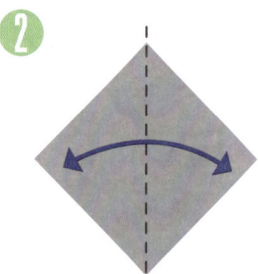
Fold in half to make a crease and unfold.

3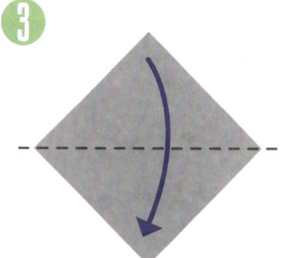
Fold in half horizontally.

4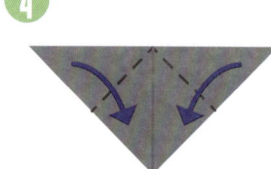
Fold in two corners of the triangle toward the center.

5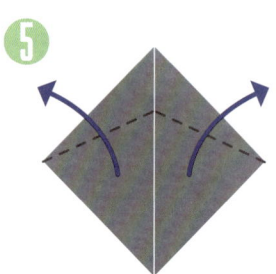
Fold upward on the dotted line.

6
Fold downward on the dotted line.

7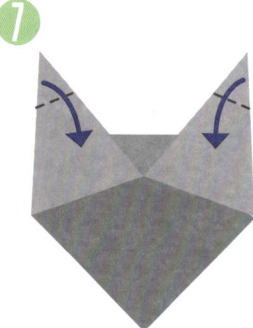
Fold downward on the dotted line.

8
Turn over.

9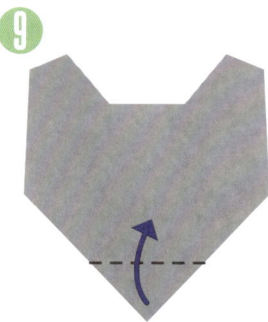
Fold one side upward on the dotted line.

10
Fold the other side upward on the dotted line.

11
Draw on a cute face and ears.

> Did you know that koalas are nocturnal? This means they are asleep in the day and awake at night.

Kind thought of the day
I can do kind things without being asked.

One-legged mindfulness!

Now that you're a master of mindfulness, try this simple exercise. See if you can balance on one leg. How long can you stay like this? Now try on the other leg. Keep doing this exercise over several days and see if each time you can balance for a little longer.

Koala facts

Koalas are found in Australia, where they live in forests and eat eucalyptus leaves. They can sleep for up to 18 hours a day. There are fewer koalas than there used to be. This is because the forests where they live are being cut down. However, there are many people, such as conservationists, who are now trying to help koalas.

Color in this page.

Well done!

Now, it's time to give yourself a big pat on the back for completing the activities.

Draw a face on the tiger to show how you feel after finishing this book.

How kind do you think you are on a scale of 1 to 10?
10 is super kind!